FLASHBACK HISTORY

PREHISTORIC PEOPLE

Susie Brooks

PowerKiDS
press.
New York

Published in 2010 by The Rosen Publishing Group, Inc.
29 East 21st Street, New York, NY 10010

Copyright © 2010 Wayland/The Rosen Publishing Group, Inc.

First Edition

Original series design: Dave West
Illustrator: Ian Thompson
Layout for this edition: Alix Wood
Editor for this edition: Katie Powell

Library of Congress Cataloging-in-Publication Data

Brooks, Susie.
Prehistoric people / Susie Brooks.
    p. cm. — (Flashback history)
  Includes index.
  ISBN 978-1-4358-5504-5 (library binding)
  ISBN 978-1-4358-5505-2 (pbk.)
  ISBN 978-1-4358-5506-9 (6-pack)
  1. Prehistoric people—Juvenile literature. I. Title.
  GN744.B76 2010
  930—dc22
                                    2009001848

Picture Credits: Front cover: English Heritage Photo Library; The Ancient Art & Architecture Collecton, p27(tl), p43(b) (Mike Andrew); Ashmolean Museum, Oxford, p20(l); The Trustees of the British Museum, p13(c), p13(t), p24(r), p30, p32(b); Butser Ancient Farm Project Rust, p14, p15; Cambridge University Museum of Archaeology and Anthropology, p27(tr), p37(t), p37(c); J.Allan Cash Photolibrary, p18, p43(tl); Sue Cunningham/Sue Cunningham Photographic, p42; English Heritage Photo Library, p23, p26/27, p40: Giraudon, p16(r), p17(l); Robert Harding Picture Library, p20(r), p21(b), p31(b) (dr Pfirrmann), p34, p36(b); Magnum, p16(l) (Steve McCurry), p17(r) (Thomas Hoepker), p18/19 (Ernst Haas), p32/33 (Rene Burri); Milwaukee Public Museum, USA, p8(l); Museum of London, p12/13, p14/15, p22/23(t), p40/41; The Museum of the Wiltshire Archaeological and Natural History Society, Devizes, p31(c); National Museum of Greenland, p25; National Museum of Ireland, Dublin, p35(b), p36(t); Natural History Museum, London, p28(r); Office of Public Works, Ireland, p32(t); Phoebe Hearst Museum of Anthropology, The University of California at Berkeley, p29, p35(t); Picturepoint, p19, p22/23(b), p27(b), p31(t), p43(tr), Salisbury and South Wiltshire Museum, p8(r), p37(b) (English Heritage Photolibrary); Somerset Levels Project, p38 (Dr J.M. Coles); Roger Vlitos, p32(c); Werner Foreman Archive, p9, p29; Field Museum of Natural History, Chicago, p21(c) and p21(cr); British Museum, London, p22; Auckland Institute and Museum, Auckland, p24(l) Soc.Polymathique du Morbihan, p28(l) Centennial Museum, Vancouver, p38/39; Museum Fur Volkerkunder, Berlin, p41; Hermitage Museum, Leningrad; Zefa, endpapers.

Manufactured in China.

Endpapers: Enormous statues made in about 1000 AD by the people of the Easter Island in the Pacific Ocean.

CONTENTS

Words that appear in **BOLD** can be found in the glossary on page 44.

WHO WERE THE PREHISTORIC PEOPLE?

The word *prehistoric* describes a time long ago, before history was first written

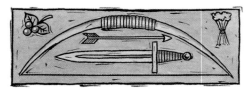

down. People began to record history at different times in different places. The Sumerians in the Middle East, for example, invented writing in around 3000 BCE. But in Australia, there are no written records until after 1600 CE. This means that the dates of prehistory vary around the world.

GATHERING CLUES ◀ ▼

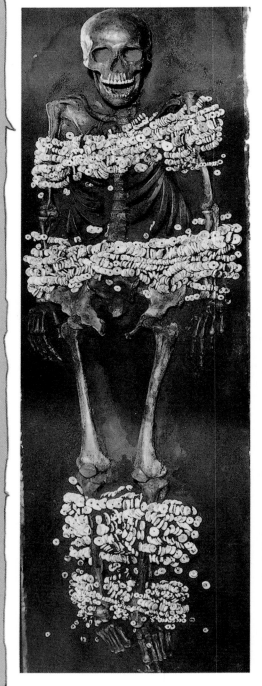

The clues we have about life in prehistoric times include clothes, tools, and even whole buildings. There are also bones. The skeleton on the left, found in the U.S., is from around 1200 CE. **Archaeologists** think that it belonged to a princess, because she was buried with lots of valuable shell beads. The bones below, from England, date back to about 2000 BCE. This man was buried with a drinking pot and a dagger. They were probably meant to help him in the **afterlife**.

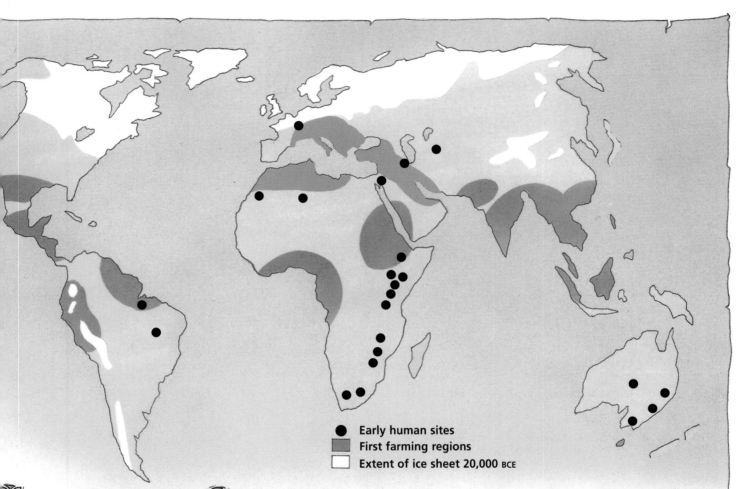

Early human sites
First farming regions
Extent of ice sheet 20,000 BCE

ARCHAEOLOGY

Archaeologists have to be very careful when they uncover ancient finds. Items that have been lying underground for thousands of years can be extremely fragile. Not everything survives. For example, the skeletons on the left would have been buried in clothes, but these have rotted away. The **bronze** blade of the man's dagger remains, but its wooden handle does not. Experts have to do a lot of detective work. They make detailed records and use special techniques to work out dates and fill in missing information.

DEVELOPING HUMANS

Human beings have been around for much longer than most people think. An early type of person, called a hominid, developed in Africa possibly 7 million years ago. Archaeologists have found actual footprints that are more than 3.5 million years old. Another type of human, called *Homo habilis*, also lived in Africa around 2.5 million years ago. This was followed by *Homo erectus*, whose remains were found later in Asia. An early hunter type called *Homo neanderthalis* developed in Europe from about 400,000 years ago. *Homo sapiens* is the name for modern humans, believed to have existed for nearly 200,000 years.

CRAFT SKILLS ▼

This copper-crafted bird with a pearl for an eye is an example of prehistoric work. It was made by someone from a farming community in North America, in around 100 BCE.

TIMELINE

	900,000-100,000 BCE	100,000-8000 BCE	8000-5000 BCE	5000 BCE-0	0-600 CE
EVENTS IN AFRICA	200,000–100,000 BCE Early forms of *Homo sapiens* develop in eastern and southern Africa.	10,000 BCE After the last Ice Age, people live and hunt in the Sahara region of Africa.	6500 BCE Cattle are bred in Africa.	4000 BCE **Millet** and **sorghum** are grown in Sudan.	400 Towns appear south of the Sahara desert. 600 The Kingdom of Ghana is the first state in West Africa. Rock art
EVENTS IN ASIA AND AUSTRALASIA	900,000 BCE Early hominids live in western Asia. Around 600,000 BCE Early *Homo erectus* live in China. Around 150,000 BCE Neanderthal peoples live in western Asia.	70,000–50,000 BCE Humans arrive in Australia. About 11,000 BCE Wheat is first harvested in Syria. 9000 BCE Sheep are first farmed in the Middle East.	8000 BCE Jericho, in the Middle East, has an organized farming community. 7000 BCE Wheat, barley, and pigs are farmed in Anatolia (Turkey).	4500 BCE Farming begins around the River Ganges, India. 1500 BCE People begin writing in China.	650 People settle in Polynesia in the Pacific. **Early writing**
EVENTS IN EUROPE	900,000 BCE Early hominids are already living in Europe. 600,000 BCE The first hand axes are used. 300,000 BCE Hunters settle by lakes in Germany.	45,000 BCE Modern humans arrive in Europe during the last Ice Age. 30,000 BCE The first European cave paintings are made.	6500 BCE Farms appear in the Balkans (southeastern Europe). Melted ice separates Britain from Europe. 5200 BCE Farming spreads north to the Netherlands.	4500 BCE **Megalithic** tombs are made in western Europe. 4000 BCE Flint mines appear. 3500 BCE Simple plows are first used in northern and western Europe.	43 The Romans invade and take over Britain. 476 The Western Roman Empire falls when the last emperor, Romulus Augustus, is removed from power.
EVENTS IN THE AMERICAS	**North American hut**	30,000 BCE People arrive in Alaska from Asia.	8000 BCE New types of stone tools appear. 7000 BCE The first crops are grown in Mexico. 6300 BCE Grain and potatoes are grown in Peru.	5000 BCE People begin planting crops in the Amazon. 1200 BCE Civilized societies develop in Central America.	300 The Maya civilization reaches its peak in Central America.

Flint

600-1450	1450-1650	1650-1890	1890-2009
1434 onward The Portuguese discover various parts of West Africa.	1487–8 The Portuguese explorer, Bartolomeu Dias, sails around the Cape of Good Hope, southern Africa.	1652 The Dutch East India Company forms a **settlement** in Cape Town.	1948 South Africa introduces apartheid, a system that separates the lives of white and black people. 1990 Apartheid comes to an end.

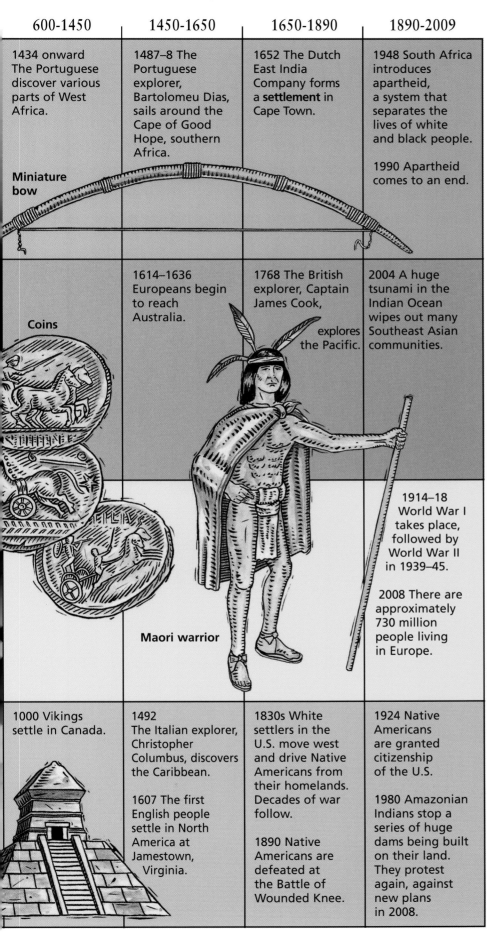

Miniature bow

Coins

Maori warrior

| | 1614–1636 Europeans begin to reach Australia. | 1768 The British explorer, Captain James Cook, explores the Pacific. | 2004 A huge tsunami in the Indian Ocean wipes out many Southeast Asian communities. 1914–18 World War I takes place, followed by World War II in 1939–45. 2008 There are approximately 730 million people living in Europe. |

| 1000 Vikings settle in Canada. | 1492 The Italian explorer, Christopher Columbus, discovers the Caribbean. 1607 The first English people settle in North America at Jamestown, Virginia. | 1830s White settlers in the U.S. move west and drive Native Americans from their homelands. Decades of war follow. 1890 Native Americans are defeated at the Battle of Wounded Knee. | 1924 Native Americans are granted citizenship of the U.S. 1980 Amazonian Indians stop a series of huge dams being built on their land. They protest again, against new plans in 2008. |

VARIED PEOPLES

It is easy to think of prehistoric humans as being "primitive," or less advanced than people are today. In reality, they just had a very different way of life. Prehistoric peoples were not the same all over the world, but they all learned great skills to help them survive. Some slowly moved from being hunter-gatherers (see page 12) to farming and living in towns. Others continued living closely with nature, finding all they needed from the land. Although we can make good guesses about things that prehistoric people did and believed, it is impossible to know everything about them.

BCE or CE?

The letters CE stand for "Common Era," and BCE "Before the Common Era." They refer to times after and before the birth of Christ. The years BCE are counted backward.

DID PREHISTORIC PEOPLE EAT WELL?

There were no stores or supermarkets in prehistoric times. People had to find their own food. We call them hunter-gatherers, because they hunted for meat and gathered wild plants to eat. Different animals and plants fed different people all over the world. In some places, **indigenous** peoples still hunt and gather today.

Mammoth hunting

KILLING A MAMMOTH ▲

These hunters lived in North America in about 9000 BCE. The huge beast they are killing is a **mammoth,** but they also hunted bison, horses, and **tapirs**. It took several men to bring down an animal like this one. Their weapons were simple wooden spears with stone blades.

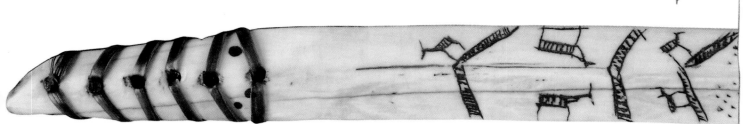

ARCTIC HUNTERS ▲

This knife is made of walrus tusk and was used by the Inuit of the Arctic. The Inuit hunted animals, such as seals and **caribou**, across the ice. They also caught fish and seabirds from fast-moving canoes called **kayaks**. Today, the Inuit have guns and snowmobiles, but some still live traditional lives.

▼ SWIMMING REINDEER

The mammoth's tusk below has been carved to show two swimming reindeer. It was found in a rock shelter in France and dates back to 10,500 BCE. In those days, people hunted huge herds of reindeer. They relied on the animals for food and used their skins and bones for clothes, tools, and weapons.

HUNTING WEAPONS ▼

Prehistoric hunters invented many types of spear and arrow. They used a wide range of materials including bone, ivory (from tusks), wood, and rock. The fishing spears below were carved from antlers about 10,000 years ago. The spikes would stick into the fish's flesh. A new wooden handle has been attached to the bottom spear.

FISHING AND COLLECTING

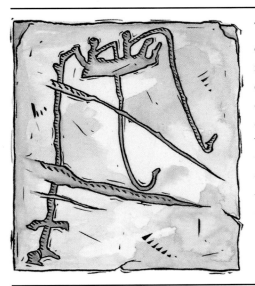

This drawing of a rock carving from Sweden shows two fishermen in a boat. Can you see the anchor and fishing lines dangling down? When they weren't fishing or hunting, prehistoric peoples collected foods such as edible roots, wild oats, honey, nettles, nuts, and berries. They also caught small animals, such as lizards, for snacks.

WHO GREW FOOD IN PREHISTORIC TIMES?

In the prehistory of the world, there were several long, very cold periods called Ice Ages. The last one ended in about 10000 BCE. As the ice melted, there was a lot more rain and the warmer climate produced new plants. People in the Middle East found that they could replant wild seeds on the **fertile** land. This was how farming began.

A WORLD OF CROPS

The world's first crops were early forms of wheat and barley, grown by the Middle Eastern farmers. In about 8300 BCE, people in Peru planted wild grasses and beans. By 6000 BCE, the Chinese were farming rice and millet, and in Mexico people began harvesting corn in about 5000 BCE. Other crops grown by prehistoric peoples included root vegetables, potatoes, and sorghum.

PLOWING THE LAND ▲ ▶

To help farmers prepare the land for **sowing**, some prehistoric peoples discovered how to plow. The farmers above are recreating a type of plowing used in prehistoric Britain. On the right you can see copies of Swedish rock carvings, showing farmers and animals working the fields.

Plowing

In a peat bog in Tollund, Denmark, two villagers made an amazing find—the body of a prehistoric man, complete with his last meal! The waterlogged soil helped to preserve the corpse for around 2,400 years. Inside his stomach is a thin gruel or soup, made from ingredients such as those shown on the right. Archaeologists have since tried the recipe— apparently it didn't taste very nice!

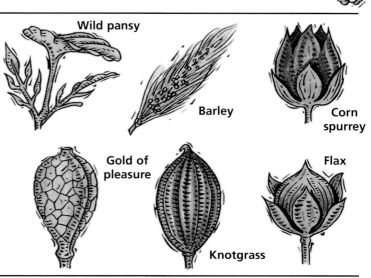

Wild pansy

Barley

Corn spurrey

Gold of pleasure

Flax

Knotgrass

◀ FARMING TOOLS

Axes like this one were used in Europe and Asia to clear forests for farming. This ancient flint blade has been bound to a wooden handle for display in a modern museum. Experiments have shown that you can cut down a narrow tree in seven minutes using this axe. Other farming tools included hoes and spades for shifting soil. Most of the fields that prehistoric farmers worked in were small.

FARM ANIMALS ▼

The first farm animals were sheep, introduced in Iraq and Iran in around 9000 BCE. Goats came slightly later, then pigs around 7000 BCE in Turkey. Cattle were farmed in northern Africa and the Mediterranean from about 6000 BCE. The sheep on the right are soay—first bred in Europe before Roman times. Elsewhere, prehistoric people raised all kinds of animals including horses, chickens, turkeys, guinea pigs, and **llamas**.

DID THEY HAVE FAMILIES LIKE OURS?

Prehistoric peoples left behind clues that tell us they lived in family groups. There are statues like the ones below, and cemeteries containing adult and child remains. We can also learn a lot from their modern-day relations—indigenous peoples such as the Native Americans, Maoris, and Aboriginals.

AN ABORIGINAL FAMILY ▼

Aboriginal people have lived in Australia for tens of thousands of years. Traditionally, they were hunter-gatherers. They moved around in groups of about 30 people, which included several families. An Aboriginal man could have more than one wife and many children.

WHAT DID THEY LOOK LIKE? ▲ ▶

These clay figures were made in Romania about 6,000 years ago. They give us a basic picture of a prehistoric woman (right) and man (above). Sometimes scientists can work out people's facial details from their skeletons.

16

HARD WORKERS ▶

This drawing was copied from an 8,000-year-old rock painting in Spain. It shows a woman scooping wild honey from a beehive in a tree. Men, women, and children all worked in prehistoric times.

POWERFUL WOMEN

Lots of evidence suggests that women were as important, if not more important, than men in some prehistoric groups. Often it was women who:
• gathered most of the food
• learned how to plant crops
• were rulers, such as in **Celtic** tribes.

CHILDCARE ▶

This modern Aboriginal mother is making a traditional cradle. In prehistoric times, in hunter-gatherer groups, women took children with them on food collecting trips or left them at home with an elderly relative.

WHERE DID PREHISTORIC PEOPLE LIVE?

Prehistoric people were always traveling in search of food, so the first people didn't live in houses. Instead, they made temporary shelters, something like tents. When people discovered farming, they started to settle in villages and

later towns. They learned how to build strong homes out of timber and stone—and how to heat them in the winter.

MOBILE HOMES ▶

One of the first clues about prehistoric housing comes from northern Europe about 12,000 years ago. Here, people used mammoth bones as tent poles and covered them with animal skins. These early shelters probably looked a little like **tepees**, used by Native American hunters.

CAVE DWELLING ▼

In Europe and the Americas, caves also made handy homes. This cliff shelter was used by traveling hunters in France about 12,000 years ago. They probably added walls made of wood and animal skins. Inside, they would light a fire for warmth, cooking—and to keep wild animals out!

At Skara Brae on the Scottish Island of Orkney, you can visit a village built in 3100 BCE. The round, stone houses were joined by covered passageways. Their roofs were thatched with turf and heather over beams of wood or whalebone. Inside, the furniture was made from slabs of stone.

On the far left is a bed that would have been filled with soft heather for a mattress. In the center of the room is a hearth for a fire. The kitchen area (bottom right) includes a watertight container for keeping shellfish and a stone for grinding grain. Around the walls are built-in cupboards and dressers.

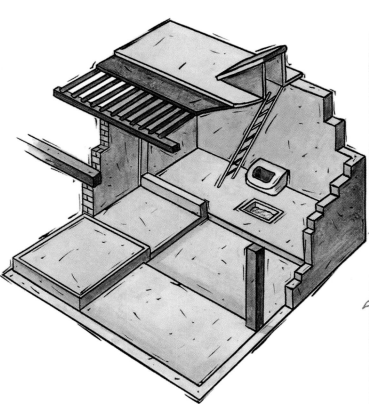

TOWN HOUSE ▲

This drawing shows a house in one of the first farming settlements, at Çatal Hüyük in Turkey. In 7000 BCE, there was a village here, but by 6000 BCE it had become a busy town. The houses were all linked and there were no front doors, just ladders coming down from the roof. Each house had one big room, with raised areas for sleeping.

COULD PREHISTORIC PEOPLE READ AND WRITE?

Since prehistory was before written records, you would expect there to be no writing. However some prehistoric peoples did use symbols to show various actions and ideas. Many of these are hard to understand today, but surviving groups, such as the Aboriginals, have told us what some of them mean.

ANCIENT GREEK ▲

At the end of the prehistoric period, people began to develop writing. This early form of Greek is from the island of Crete. The Greeks who conquered Crete in around 1450 BCE kept records on clay **tablets**. These included little pictures, or **pictograms**, of animals, food, and equipment. Although some of the symbols are unrecognizable, you can see things like chariot wheels quite clearly. Experts call this style of writing "Linear B."

TRADEMARKS ▶

The three **seals** to the right came from Mohenjo-daro, the first city in India, about 4,500 years ago. They were used on crates of goods and probably show the names of merchant traders. The animals may be trademarks, or logos, of different companies.

Prehistoric peoples had languages, even if they did not write them down. The Inuit's spoken language was only turned into writing when Europeans visited the Arctic. They became interested in Inuit words and **dialects** and decided to give them an alphabet. In Canada, they wrote in symbols called syllabics, and in Greenland, letters like ours were used. Nanuq is the Inuit word for polar bear; arlu means killer whale.

SIOUX CALENDAR ▲

The buffalo-skin calendar above was painted by a Sioux Indian. The symbols show events that his tribe experienced from 1800 to 1872. They include war, diseases, and even an eclipse of the sun.

▲ NAMES ON COINS

Here you can see both sides of a coin made in prehistoric Britain. It is a gold coin of the Celtic leader, Cunobelinus, who died in around 40 CE. The writing is in Latin, which uses V instead of U. Look for letters from the leader's name and from his capital, Camulodunum.

WHAT WORK DID PREHISTORIC PEOPLE DO?

Most work in prehistoric times involved making things or finding or growing food. As groups and settlements became bigger, some jobs needed specialists to work at them full-time. In northern Europe, for example, huge amounts of flint were used to make tools for clearing land. So some people became flint miners, spending their days digging underground.

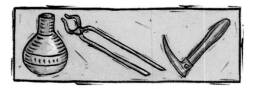

SPINNING THREAD ▶

Tools give us some of the most important clues about the work that prehistoric people did. Here, you can see a spindle, used for spinning wool into thread. At the end is a round, clay weight called a whorl, which allows the spindle to turn. This one was used in Britain more than 2,000 years ago. The wooden shaft rotted and has been replaced.

◀ MAORI TAILORING

Making clothes was an important task that involved all kinds of materials. This Maori cloak was woven from the **fibers** of the **flax** plant. People scraped, dried, and twisted the flax leaves to make patterns or threads. Sometimes pieces were dyed with plant coloring.

DIGGING FOR FLINT ▲

Around 3500 BCE, the first farmers in Britain discovered that flint from the surface of the ground was too weak to make good axes. So they started to dig underground using deer antler picks. They became the first miners, digging down as deep as 40 feet (12 meters) through layers of soil and chalk.

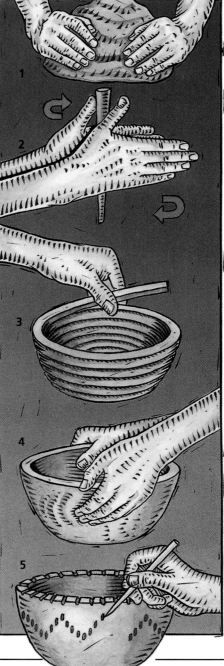

The first clay pots were probably made about 10,000 years ago. Clay is a type of earth, dug from the ground.

First the potter kneaded the clay to make it supple and remove any air bubbles (1).

To make a coil pot, long sausages of clay were rolled and then laid in a spiral (2 and 3).

Next, the potter smoothed the sides, inside and out and then heated the pot (4).

For decoration, a stick could be used to make patterns (5). Other designs were created using twisted cord, fingernails, or bones sometimes shaped into combs.

MINE SHAFT ▶

On the right is part of a flint mine in England. Miners dug tunnels like these to get as much flint as they could. The tunnels had to be quite small so that the roof did not collapse. Pillars of chalk were left as props, but the iron ones in this photograph are modern.

WHAT DID PREHISTORIC PEOPLE WEAR?

Animal skins, plant fibers, and tree roots were used for making clothes. Many prehistoric peoples used bone or wooden needles for sewing. Farmers wove cloth and dyed it with plant colors, such as yellow from pine cones.

JEWELRY ▲

Prehistoric people all around the world wore jewelry. This bracelet was made in France around 600 BCE, out of seven pressed bronze rings. Often, people used much simpler seed beads or shells.

COSTUME ▶

This decorative costume was worn at a funeral in Tahiti. The cloth, made from tree bark, is decorated with feathers and pearly shells. Prehistoric clothing often had to be pinned in place. The elaborate brooch below might have held together a cloak.

Celtic brooch

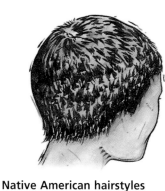

Native American hairstyles

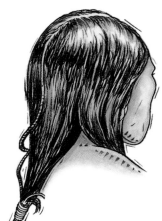
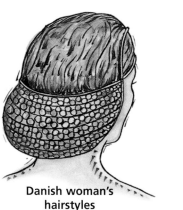

Danish woman's hairstyles

HAIRSTYLES ▲

These drawings were made from people's hair that has actually survived. The heads of these Native Americans were preserved in dry, sandy graves for about 1,500 years. The woman's hairnet was found in peat from prehistoric Denmark.

THE ICE MAN

In 1991, the 5,300-year-old body of a hunter was found in a **glacier** in the European Alps. Only small parts of his clothing survived, but this drawing shows what archaeologists think he looked like. His animal-skin clothes and boots were lined with grass for warmth, and he wore a bear-fur hat. He carried a wooden-framed backpack and a pouch that held flints and sticks for making a fire.

▲ INUIT MUMMIES

This Inuit baby is a naturally formed **mummy**—one of eight found in Qilakitsoq, Greenland. They were probably buried in 1475, but their faces and warm sealskin clothing lasted in the cold, dry air.

WHAT DID PREHISTORIC PEOPLE WORSHIP?

We know from surviving peoples that their prehistoric **ancestors** worshiped various gods and spirits. The dead were often buried with their belongings, showing that they believed in an afterlife. Some statues and stone carvings show religious rituals, too.

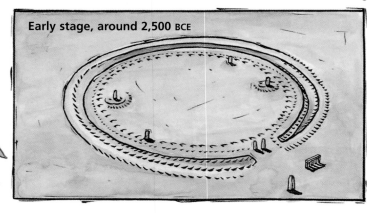

Early stage, around 2,500 BCE

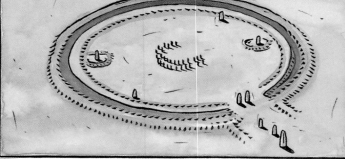

Bluestones are brought from Wales, 124 miles (200 kilometers) away, around 2150 BCE

STONEHENGE

The famous stone circle at Stonehenge, England, was started in 3000 BCE. We think it was some kind of temple, or even a magical healing place. Everything was carefully measured so that on the summer **solstice**, the sun rises through the entrance. Building Stonehenge was a massive task, with stones weighing up to 50 tonnes. You can see different stages of its construction on the left.

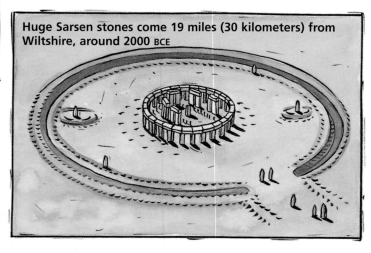

Huge Sarsen stones come 19 miles (30 kilometers) from Wiltshire, around 2000 BCE

◄ ART OR MAGIC?

This French cave painting shows a bison with arrows and wounds. Pictures like this may have been part of special rituals to bring success in hunting.

MOTHER GODDESS ►

Many statues like this one have been found dating from 25,000 to 10,000 BCE. They are thought to be fertility goddesses, perhaps meant to encourage births.

ASTER ISLAND STATUES ►

These huge statues have stood on Easter Island, in the Pacific, for more than 1,000 years. They all face the sun—perhaps the early islanders worshiped the sun? Did the statues represent gods, or people's ancestors made into gods? No one is sure.

DID PREHISTORIC PEOPLE GO TO THE DOCTOR?

Prehistoric people did not have the benefit of modern hospitals and medicines, but they did go to the doctor. They knew about natural cures from plants, and also how to fix broken bones. They even performed complicated and dangerous surgery.

▼ SKULL SURGERY

This 2,000 year-old skull of a Native American has been operated on twice. You can see where small pieces of the bone have been cut out. This operation was called *trepanation* and could be used to treat headaches and epilepsy. It often had a spiritual link, for example, to cure diseases by letting evil spirits escape.

Tooth taken out and hole healed up

Tooth very worn

Abscess under tooth

TOOTHY TALE ▶

The owner of this jawbone lived in Britain around 2000 BCE. He seems to have had a tooth removed. Archaeologists can tell how old someone was and what type of diet they ate by looking at a skeleton's teeth.

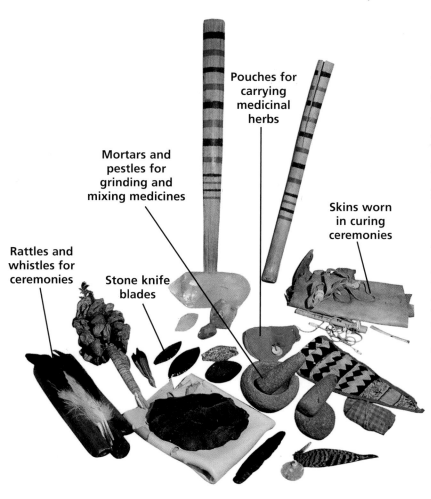

Mortars and pestles for grinding and mixing medicines

Pouches for carrying medicinal herbs

Skins worn in curing ceremonies

Rattles and whistles for ceremonies

Stone knife blades

◀ MEDICINE MEN

Many Native American tribes appointed skilled medicine men to cure their ills. These supplies belonged to a Miwok healer from California, who used them in special ceremonies.

NATURAL CURES ▼

Natural cures were popular in prehistoric times, just as they are today. The farmers at Skara Brae (see page 19) used the plants below.

Puff-ball—to stop bleeding

BURIALS

When archaeologists **excavate** cemeteries, they can often find out lots of information about the health and size of a group of people. The bones themselves can give away certain diseases, such as **leprosy** or arthritis. They may also reveal injuries from battle, or fractures that have not healed. The drawing on the left is a copy of a skeleton from Britain. It belonged to a child of about 13, who was buried with a pot under a mound of earth nearly 4,000 years ago.

Henbane—for toothache, general aches and to help with sleep

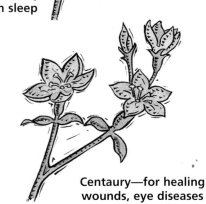

Centaury—for healing wounds, eye diseases and snake bites

WHO WERE THE PREHISTORIC RULERS?

There were many different types of ruler in prehistoric times, just as there are today. We have evidence that some groups were led by kings, others by chiefs, some were ruled by women and others by men. One of the most famous female rulers was Boudicca of eastern Britain. She led a great uprising against the Romans in about 60 CE.

OBJECTS OF POWER ▼

Surviving objects can tell us a lot about the importance of their owners. This beaten gold cup was made with great skill and care. It was found with a skeleton in southwestern Britain, dating back to about 1500 BCE. No one knows the name of the person, but he or she must have ranked highly to be buried with such a precious object.

Umbrella top

STATUS SYMBOLS ▲

A status symbol is something that displays a person's wealth or social position. An example today might be an expensive car or a very grand house. The umbrella top above belonged to an Asante king or chieftain in Ghana, West Africa. It was one of many royal status symbols, which also included an important golden stool.

◀ A BRITISH LEADER

This statue is of the Iceni tribe leader—Boudicca. She was described as: *"A very big woman, terrifying to look at, with a fierce look on her face. She had a harsh voice and wore her hair—the color of a lion's mane—right down to her hips. She used to brandish her spear to strike terror into the hearts of her warriors."*

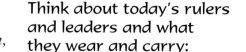

RULERS TODAY

Think about today's rulers and leaders and what they wear and carry:

• Military leaders wear different uniforms from other soldiers, to show their rank.

• Judges still wear long wigs in many countries such as the U.K.

• Kings and queens have crowns and elaborate costumes for important occasions. Sometimes they carry special objects like the prehistoric mace below.

Gold ornaments

Daggers

Mace

Axe

BURIED WITH A LEADER ▲

The objects above probably belonged to a British leader, buried in about 2000 BCE. The mace was a status object, made from a wooden handle with a stone end.

CHIEF'S HEADDRESS ▶

This Kiowa Indian chieftain wears a warrior headdress. Status symbols like this have been worn by Native Americans for hundreds of years.

WERE THERE ARTISTS IN PREHISTORIC TIMES?

There were many skilled artists and craftspeople in prehistoric times. They did not paint pictures to hang in galleries, but art was part of their everyday lives. Often, the carvings, drawings, and other decorative work they made had special meaning.

◀ ART OR SYMBOLS?

This carving was made in about 3000 BCE inside a huge burial mound at Newgrange in Ireland. The spirals are mysterious, but some people think they represent the journey to the next world.

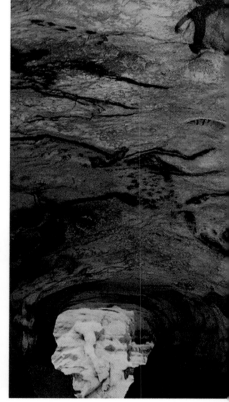

COWBOY, BY AN INDIAN ▶

In the 1800s, Navajo Indians in the Southwest painted records of various events. This one in Canyon de Chelly shows a white-skinned cowboy on horseback. In the same area, there are rock paintings by earlier peoples, living up to 2,000 years ago.

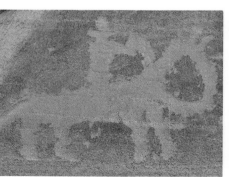

CHEROKEE CRAFT ▶

A Cherokee Indian wove this basket by hand in the 1700s. It is made of split cane, dyed with plant colorings.

ANCIENT TATTOOS ▶

This illustration shows a piece of tattooed skin from around 400 BCE. It came from a grave in Siberia, Russia, where the frozen ground preserved the dead bodies in amazing detail.

Tattoo

AFRICAN CAVE ART ▼

Paintings like the one below were made about 6,000 years ago in the Sahara region of Africa. This desert area was much wetter then, and people could farm cattle there.

MAKE YOUR OWN CAVE ART

This hunting scene is one of a series of famous paintings in the caves at Lascaux, France. It was made in about 15,000 BCE, using paints mixed from natural materials. The artists probably used sticks, plants stems, and tufts of hair or fur as paintbrushes. It was tricky to work on the rough walls. You could try it for yourself using a piece of thick cardboard. Crumple it up, then open it out again. Now try painting on it with your fingers, a twig, sponges, or even a feather. Experiment with different types of paint.

WHAT DID THEY DO IN THEIR SPARE TIME?

It seems that music has always been an important part of human life. Archaeologists have found ancient musical instruments and paintings that show people dancing. Storytelling was also popular in prehistoric times—without it, many tales and traditions would have been lost.

◀ DANCING GIRL

This delicate bronze dancing girl was sculpted in Mohenjo-daro, India, in around 2500 BCE. She is wearing nothing but a necklace and a long set of armlets. Perhaps she danced to entertain, or as part of a ceremony.

▼ ANIMAL BELLS

Many prehistoric farmers hung bells like these around their cows' and goats' necks. It helped them to keep track of the animals—and they probably enjoyed the jingling music, too!

African animal bells

Lyre or harp

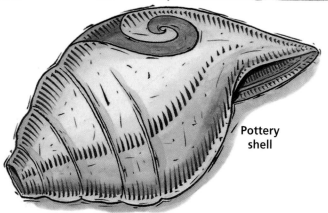
Pottery
shell

HELL SOUNDS ▲

Musicians could make all kinds of sounds
by blowing into seashells. Around 100 CE,
the Moche people of Peru made pottery shells
to use as musical instruments.

DEER BONE GAME ▶

Animal bones were always useful for making
things. This game was made out of deer bones
and played by the Wailaki Indians from California.

MUSICAL INSTRUMENTS

This lyre, or small harp, survived in the same
tomb as the tattooed skin on page 33. It was
made in about 400 BCE, from wood with a
stretched leather cover. Simpler prehistoric
instruments included: drums, metal
rattles, bone flutes, and discs
threaded with string, which
buzzed when twirled.

IRISH HORN ▼

Some prehistoric people buried objects
for safekeeping. These bronze items were
hidden under Irish soil for nearly 3,000 years.
The horn can still be played—it makes deep,
loud notes.

DID PREHISTORIC PEOPLE INVENT THINGS?

Humans have always invented things to try to solve their problems. In prehistoric times, people first needed to work out how to survive—and then how to make life

better. They invented tools for hunting, building, and eventually farming. They also discovered how to tame animals, grow crops, and transport things around.

◄ CLAY POTS

It was hard to get by without containers! Prehistoric people used their imagination and made boxes and baskets out of bark, leaves, leather, bone, and stone. About 10,000 years ago, people discovered how to fire clay to make it hard. These decorated clay pots were buried with people in Ireland in about 2000 BCE.

INVENTING THE WHEEL ▶

The wheel was a VERY important invention—we still use it every day. The first wheel was probably made in the Middle East more than 5,000 years ago, by people called the Sumerians. Early wheels were solid, but later, spokes were added. On the right is a model of an Indian cart, from around 2500 BCE. In some places, traditional vehicles like this are still used.

DISCOVERING METALS ▼ ▶

The discovery of metal around 7000 BCE meant that tools no longer had to be made of stone. The first metalworkers used copper, which was beaten into shape. Then they realized they could melt it and pour it into molds. Gold, bronze, and later iron, were also worked in this way. The mold below was used for making pins, about 3,000 years ago.

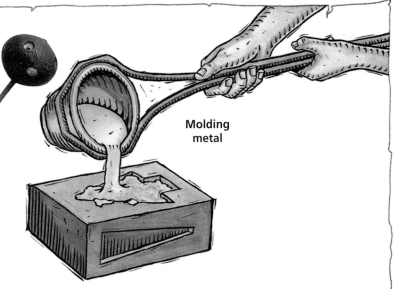

Molding metal

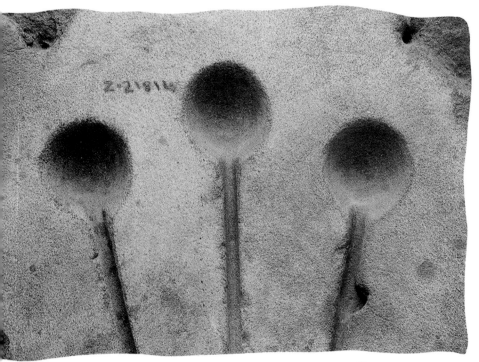

USING FLINT ▼

People first used flint to make tools at least 2.5 million years ago. Early tools were simple chunks of flint with sharp, broken edges. Then people learned to shape them for an easier grip. Flint is very hard and had to be chipped at with another stone, wood, or bone. Flakes of flint made fine blades and arrowheads, like the ones below.

OLD... AND NEW

flint tree axe	chainsaw
clay cooking pot	pan
bow and arrows	gun
dugout canoe	motorboat
plant-fiber fishing line	nylon fishing line

Making flint tools

DID PREHISTORIC PEOPLE GO ON LONG JOURNEYS?

Travel was important to prehistoric people. Hunters had to follow herds of animals, and farmers had to search for fertile land. Some people made journeys to sacred places such as Stonehenge in Britain. Roads, boats, and ships were all prehistoric inventions, and about 6,000 years ago, the Russians tamed the horse. Finally, the wheel got people moving all around the world.

TRACKS ▼

This wooden trackway in southwestern Britain was once 1.5 miles (2.5 kilometers) long. Paths like this were built from about 3500 BCE, to cross low-lying marshy land. They were discovered in modern times by people digging up peat.

▲ CARTS AND WAGONS

This drawing is a copy of a Swedish carving, made about 2,500 years ago. It shows a cart or wagon being pulled by two strong oxen. The four wheels and the animals' legs are pictured side-on, but the rest looks like a view from above.

38

HUNTING TRIPS ▶

Many prehistoric hunters tracked animals across very long distances. This picture was copied from a carving in northwest Russia. The hunter is on skis, chasing an elk or moose across the ice.

TRAVEL BY SEA ▼

Boats were invented long before any other vehicle. The earliest types were canoes dug out of tree trunks. Some prehistoric peoples in the Pacific put two canoes together and sailed up to 18,640 miles (30,000 kilometers) from island to island. The model below is of a Maori canoe in New Zealand. In real life, boats like this would have carried warriors to attack their enemies.

ACROSS THE ICE ▼

In prehistoric times, great ice sheets covered much of Russia, Scandinavia, and North America. So the people there invented skis, snowshoes, and sleds. Inuit hunters used sleds to carry heavy loads. This one is made of wood and ivory. At first, sleds were pulled by hand, but later, the Inuit trained dogs to do the job.

DID PREHISTORIC PEOPLE GO TO WAR?

When people were mainly hunter-gatherers, life was probably very peaceful. But when they started to farm and own the land, fighting and wars began to break out  about who owned the land. Archaeologists have found remains of prehistoric weapons and armor. There are also signs of towns and villages being protected against attack.

 ## DEFENDING A TOWN

Around 700 BCE, Celtic people in Britain started building towns on hilltops. One of these was Maiden Castle, whose remains you can see below. The town was circled by huge banks and ditches, measuring 46 feet (14 meters) from top to bottom. On top of the banks, there would have been strong walls.

Any enemy hoping to attack Maiden Castle had to enter through a maze of banks and tunnels. Meanwhile, people defending the town could shoot from above using slings and stones. A store has been found containing 20,000 pieces of stone ammunition.

Sheath

SHEATH AND DAGGER ▲

This sheath was a case for the dagger (right). This weapon was used by a Celtic warrior in Britain 2,000 years ago. The top of the dagger handle is carved with a human face.

A BATTLE SCENE ▼

You can see a war scene on this beautiful gold comb, which was found in a grave in southern Russia. It shows prehistoric people called the Scythians in about 500 BCE. The Scythians were known for their skill with horses and for fighting wars.

Dagger

A MAORI DEFENSE ▼

These Maori warriors are protecting their village, which would have been raised on a hill. They are standing on wooden lookout platforms, ready to face the enemy. The Maori word for a fortified place like this is *pa*.

WAGING WAR ▶

Celtic warriors often fought from chariots and horses. They protected their bodies with helmets and shields. Spears and swords were also used by prehistoric people.

WHAT HAPPENED TO PREHISTORIC PEOPLE?

Prehistoric people did not suddenly disappear—they just moved into history. Many written records began with the **Roman Empire**. People across Europe, for example, started writing when the Romans took over their lands. In other places, such as Africa, the Americas, and Australia, prehistory lasted much longer. Written records only arrived there when explorers came from Europe just a few hundred years ago.

Areas showing hunter-gatherers today

PEOPLE AT RISK
Today, there are far fewer indigenous peoples than there used to be. In the last few centuries they have suffered from slavery, war, and disease, and many have lost their traditions.

◀ CHANGING LIVES
These Kayapo Indians have been affected by the modern world—one of them is wearing a watch. But they still fight to protect their age-old way of life in the Amazon rainforest.

◀ MAORIS TODAY

The first Maoris arrived in New Zealand in around 800 CE. They lived undisturbed until 1642, when Europeans began to settle on the island. After that, their lifestyle had to change. Some Maoris, like this woman, still live in traditional villages. They are trying not to let their customs disappear.

NATIVE AMERICANS ▶

In the 1800s, white settlers spread across North America and ended the freedom of native tribes. Thousands of Native Americans were killed by disease and war. Today, many surviving tribes are living on reservations and returning to traditional ways of life.

REBUILDING

Archaeologists can help to keep prehistory alive by using pieces of evidence to reconstruct the past. This is a reconstruction of a village and trackway, built by the first farmers at Lac de Chalain in eastern France.

GLOSSARY

AFTERLIFE Life after death. Many prehistoric peoples believed in a spirit world where their souls continued living after they died.

ANCESTOR A distant relative from many generations ago.

ARCHAEOLOGIST Someone who studies ancient cultures by digging up and examining their remains.

BRONZE A metal that is a mixture of copper and tin.

CARIBOU The most northerly member of the deer family, living in Arctic regions.

CELTIC Describing the Celts—people who lived in Europe before Roman times.

DIALECT A regional variety of a language, with its own sounds, words, and/or spellings.

EXCAVATE To carefully dig up buried objects to find out things about the past.

FERTILE Productive or able to produce.

FIBERS Fine, stringy threads found in plant stems and leaves, which can be woven or spun together.

FLAX A blue-flowered plant whose stems are used to make linen.

GLACIER A huge, slowly moving mass of ice.

INDIGENOUS Native; related to the original inhabitants of a particular place.

KAYAK A canoelike boat for one or two people using double-bladed paddles.

LEPROSY A disease of the skin and nerves that began in prehistoric times.

LLAMA A South American animal from the camel family, tamed by prehistoric people to carry loads.

MAMMOTH A very large animal from the elephant family, now extinct.

MEGALITHIC Built of very large stones.

MILLET A cereal crop grown for its edible seeds.

MUMMY A dead body that has been preserved either naturally (by extreme cold or dry heat) or deliberately by humans.

PICTOGRAM The earliest form of writing, using pictures.

ROMAN EMPIRE The period when the Romans ruled much of Europe and the far north of Africa. The empire grew out of the city of Rome, founded in around 753 BCE, and peaked between 100 and 200 CE.

SEAL A stamp showing the symbol or emblem of a person, family, or business.

SETTLEMENT A place where people live and build houses.

SOLSTICE When the sun reaches its highest and lowest point in the sky.

SORGHUM A kind of grass, collected and grown to eat.

SOWING Scattering seeds for crops. Early farmers did this by hand.

TABLET A slab of stone, wood, or metal that was engraved with symbols or writing.

TAPIR A short, strong, pig-like animal found in the Americas.

TEPEE A tent supported on wooden poles.

INDEX

Web Sites
Due to the changing nature of Internet links, PowerKids Press has developed an online list of Web sites related to the subject of this book. This site is updated regularly. Please use this link to access this list: www.powerkidslinks.com/flash/prehistoric